Michael D. Butler presents

1040IMPACT

Making an impact in the 1040 Window from Pakistan to Thailand

Christmas 2024

AF104728

- **What is the 10/40 Window?**
- **Church Planting in Pakistan**
- **Streaming the Gospel into closed nations**
- **Ending Human Trafficking in Asia**

1040.ORG
IMPACT

MICHAEL'S CORNER of the world

I always felt a call to the mission field and the 10/40 window has always been a part of my prayer time. After being in ministry in the late 80's, 90's and into 2000, feeling called into business and can now say after 20 years in business that the business and ministry have dove-tailed

together and we are stepping into our stride in Pakistan, in Thailand and soon the entire 10/40 Window.

Attending **Rhema Bible College** in Tulsa, OK in 1986, Apostle Lester Sumrall came to speak on the Rhema Campus for 3 days. This was a very special time of impartation for me as I was very familiar with Sumrall's ministry for the past six years.

At 12-years-old I felt led to donate to his Lesea Broadcasting that was starting a Christian TV station in my home area of Tulsa, OK.

36 Nations - One Call

So I had been a prayer and financial partner for years by the time I first met Brother Sumrall in person at age 18. I knew I was a part of his ministry in helping establish Christ's Kingdom on earth through my prayers and my giving. I was truly a part of everything that happend at Lesa Broadcasting with people being born again watching the Word of God being broadcast in South Bend, IN, Tulsa, OK and Honolulu Hawaii and beyond!

Each month I'd make out my $20 check and mail it into the ministry and each month I'd pray for their ministry and their outreach. I saw my dollars expand, my life prosper and my ministry flourish. No doubt the fruit we're seeing today is also part of what we sowed as a teenager. **Continued page 19**

What is the 10/40 Window?

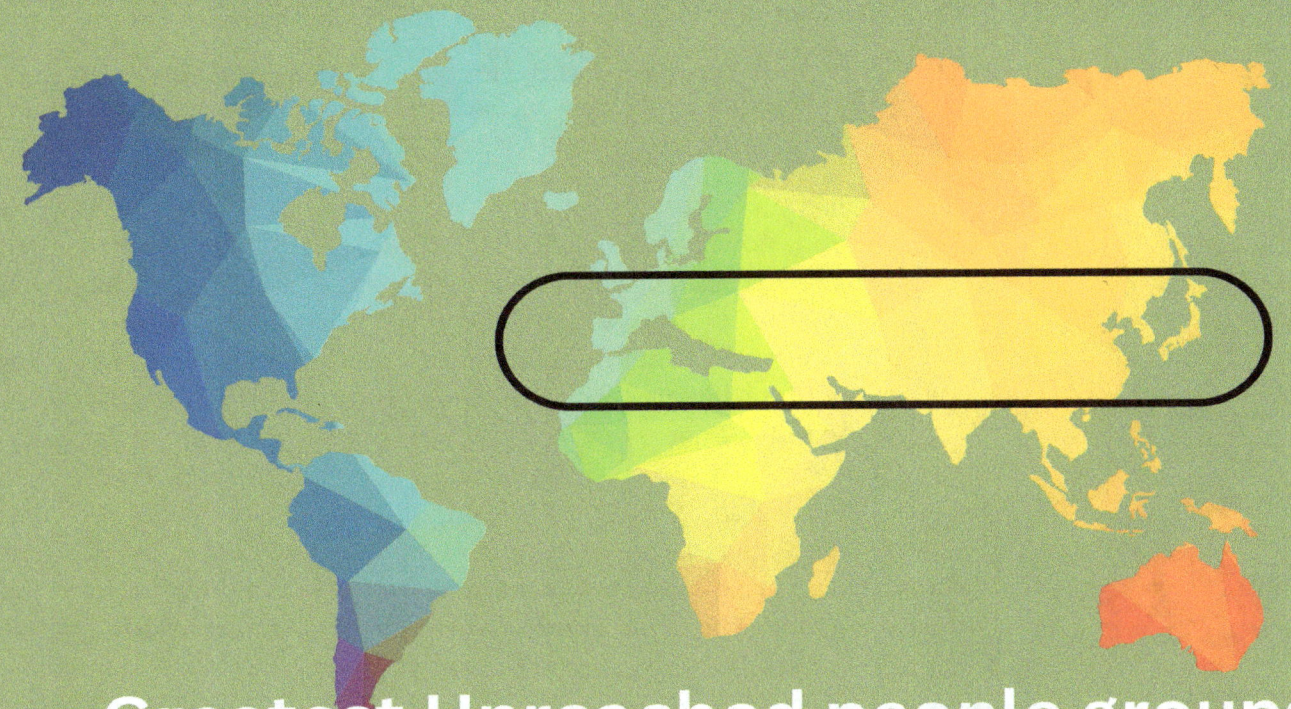

- Greatest Unreached people groups
- 5.3 Billion people (65% of world)
- 98% Muslim, Hindu & Buddists
- 3-5% Christian
- Average income $1 /day

REACHING THE UNREACHED

"And this gospel of the kingdom shall be preached in all the world for a witness unto all nations; and then shall the end come" Matthew 24:14

It's 1988 wearing my red cap and gown graduating from Rhema Bible College, hearing Pastor John Osteen deliver a powerful commencement admonition to go into all the world. Fast forward 36-years from graduating, Pastoring, Youth Pastoring, speaking in multiple countries and itinerating across the USA speaking in schools, churches, youth camps, hosting my own events and livestreaming the gospel from our TV studio in Dallas and on MichaelD.Tv.

Preaching the gospel, encouraging entrepreneurs and helping believers write and publish their books these past 36 years has taken me to: Greece, Israel, Dubai, UAE, Egypt, Puerto Rico, Estonia, London England, Brighton England, Thailand, Malaysia, Singapore, Puerto Rico, Mexico, Canada, Kuwait, Qatar, Denmark, Russia, Sweden, Colombia, South Africa, Switzerland, Pakistan and many others. The goal is to impact every nation in the 10/40 window with the gospel in their language 24/7. Our publishing company now has authors from 66 nations and I've been in 36 nations myelf traveling through half of those and speaking in half of those. We're about to livestream into all of them with the gospel and with your help!

In 2025 we'll flip the switch to be able to stream and livestream gospel content from server farms in Asia with ip addresses that are undetectable by authorities to closed nations like: China, North Korea, Saudi Arabia, Syria, India, Burma and many others. The goal is to impact every nation in the 1040 window with the gospel in their language 24/7 with 1040Tv.com

1040TV.COM
ALL THE WORLD

www.1040Tv.com

Operation Pakistan

221 CHURCHES PLANTED
4 SAFE HOUSES 416 girls rescued
27 Full-Time Staff
4 Schools
Discipleship Training
Living Water Wells/Evengelism

- 220 Million Population
- 98% Muslim
- 1% Christian
- Global Nuclear Power
- Christians are Persecuted
- Pray for the Belivers
- Help us Plant more churches &
- Train more who feel called to Preach

ENDING HUMAN TRAFFICKING-416 GIRLS RESCUED!

Imagine YOUR daughter is taken, these orphans we rescue often end up in a brothel. They have no parents. They are ages 6-17 and are forced to have sex 12-15 times a night with that many different men.

Having rescued 416 girls in the last few years, this scenerio repeats itself month after month.

The first thing they get once they are rescued is medical and trauma care, new clothes, shoes and a Bible.

We provide three meals a day and comprehensive education including: english, math, reading, writing, history, and career preparation. Our mission is to equip these young minds for life's challenges. Your support is crucial in making this mission a reality.

$400 will rescue a girl and provide for her for a full 12-months.

We invite you to consider becoming a monthly donor with contributions of $40, $100 or or $104.10 per month for the entire year. Your generosity is tax-deductible, and an impressive 96% of your gift directly supports our children, with only 4% allocated for administration.

By contributing $400, you can rescue and care for one girl from human trafficking for an entire year. However, the impact goes beyond numbers; each girl represents a changed life with a ripple effect on the future.

Thank you for donating and sharing our campaign.
GiveButter.com/1040

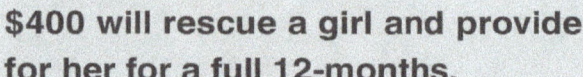

1040impact.org

Pakistan 4 Safe Houses - 416 Rescued

...She ran knowing that if she got caught she would be killed!

Mariam was promised by her traffickers that they would help her go back to school. Instead, she was sold to a brothel where she was forced to live in a room no bigger than a closet. She was brutalized by 10 men every night. Her life seemed over. BUT THAT WAS NOT THE END..

10-Year-Old Mariam's Story

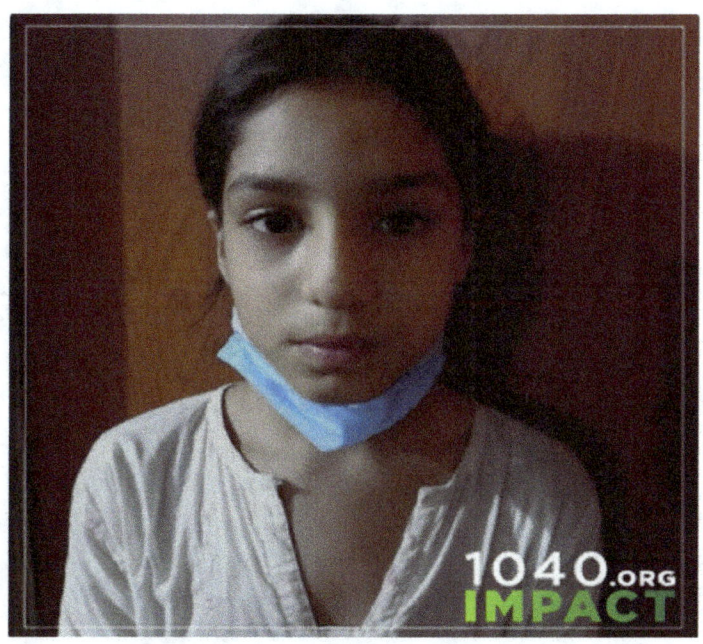

One night, her traffickers got high on drugs, and Mariam saw her opportunity. She ran for her life, knowing that if she was caught, she would be killed. Our Safe House-1040Impact team found Mariam and she is now finding her emotional and physical healing in the safety of our Safe House #2.
She is fulfilling her dream of finishing school and breaking free from a cycle of poverty and abuse,

This story can be similarly told for each of our 416 girls a few pictured below, some of them siblings.
Fifty-four of them rescued from Afghanistan when the US pulled out of the region and parents were so desperate they sold their daughters.

416 GIRLS RESCUED!

DAY TO DAY BEHIND THE SCENES

Running 1040Impact.org in Pakistan, we've rescued 416 children—mostly girls aged 6-17—from the horrors of human trafficking. After much prayer and reflection, I made the move to Southeast Asia to be closer to this vital work in August 2024. Living in the heart of the 10/40 Window, I am strategically positioned to make the greatest impact on the ground.

In Pakistan, we've established 221 churches, supported by a dedicated team of 27 full-time staff who are committed to evangelism, discipleship, and the care of our 416 children in four safe houses.

As we look to the future, we're acquiring more land to expand our reach and impact more lives, leaving a lasting, eternal legacy. But to achieve this, we need your support.

Caring for, educating, and providing for the medical, physical, and spiritual needs of these children comes with significant ongoing expenses. Beyond this, we're committed to equipping them with vocational skills, ensuring they become self-sufficient disciples who can pay their care forward and rescue others.

Being based in Asia allows me to be close to the action—to guide our team, raise the support we need, and produce documentaries that tell our story. With your partnership, we can continue this mission of hope and transformation, touching lives and making an eternal difference every day.

HELP US PRAY FOR THE 10/40 WINDOW

Join us as we pray for the 5 billion people living in the 10/40 Window, a region stretching across North Africa, the Middle East, and Asia. This area is home to the least evangelized nations in the world. Here's a breakdown:

Muslim: 60% (around 3 billion people)
Hindu: 25% (around 1.25 billion people)
Buddhist: 8% (around 400 million people)
Christian: 5% (around 250 million people)

Let's come together to pray for these diverse communities asking for open hearts to hear the Gospel and for laborers to be sent in these last days!

040Impact.org is making a difference in Pakistan and Beyond

Crusades, Church Planting, Discipelship

Speaking around the World

LIVING WATER WELLS

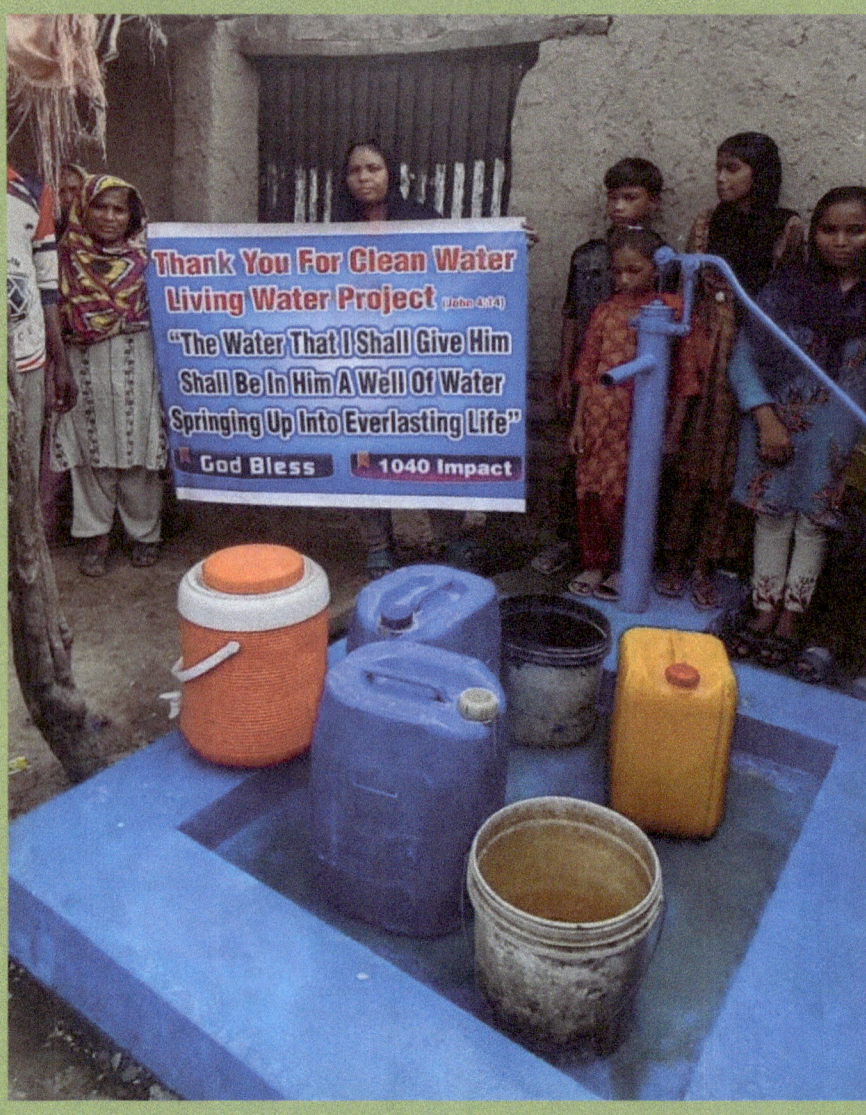

Over 22 million Pakistanis do not have access to clean drinking water. At 1040 Impact, we are committed to changing that. By drilling and installing water wells, we are providing safe, clean drinking water to 10 villages, serving over 500 people for years to come with just one well for $500.

These water wells are a life-saving resource, not just for today but for the future, ensuring sustainable access to clean water for dozens of years. Join us in our mission to make clean water accessible for all. Each water well births a church in a village giving them the living water and the natural water they need.

💧 Learn more at 1040impact.org
💧 Donate at GiveButter.com/WaterWell
We're touching hundreds of villagers with your help!

1040.ORG IMPACT

Why Thailand?

Pastor Keith Higginbotham
Bangkok, Thailand

72 Million people
98% Buddist
Close to Pakistan
Safe Environment
Affordable Overhead
Rhema Thailand - Homebase
5 Bible Schools
100 Churches

1040TV.COM
ALL THE WORLD

GO...
...PRAY
GIVE...

"*Go therefore and make disciples of all nations...*"
Matthew 28:19

1040.org
IMPACT

Become a partner

Adopt a Child
$40/month
Adopt a Child & Build
$100/month
Be a World Changer
$400/month

- Rescuing
- Feeding
- Educating

Text: 1040 to 53-555 to Donate

1040.ORG IMPACT

Israel 40-Mile Ultra Marathon

Sunday May 19 I chose to run a 40-mile ultra marathon to show my support for the hostages and to raise awareness about our non-profit in Pakistan. Meeting with the Jewish people, family members affected by the October 7th terroist attacks.

Several members of the media were my support team connecting me with the route and the support I needed on the ground to complete my mission goal. I was able to make it 40 miles instead of 56 due to blisters on my right foot.

Israel is in the 10/40 Window and is the centerpiece of God's end-time plan for the nations. We will always love Israel and pray for Israel.

Pray that the light of the glorious gospel of Christ be made real to the Jews living in Israel and those living abroad and they have a revelation of their Messiah.

Pray for the peace of Jerusalem
Psalms 122:6

"I will bless those who bless Israel" Genesis 12:3

Called to Write a Book?
Join us on our next free webinar:
BeyondWebinar.com

WHICH COUNTRY READS THE MOST?

Did you know? 76% of books in English are bought and read outside the USA

With Your Help We'll make 2025 Epic!

Adopt a child
$40/month

Adopt a child & build
$100/month

Be a World Changer
$400/month

Checks can be made to: 1040Impact and mailed to:

Bruce Butler, 3513 W. Urbana St.
Broken Arrow, OK 74012

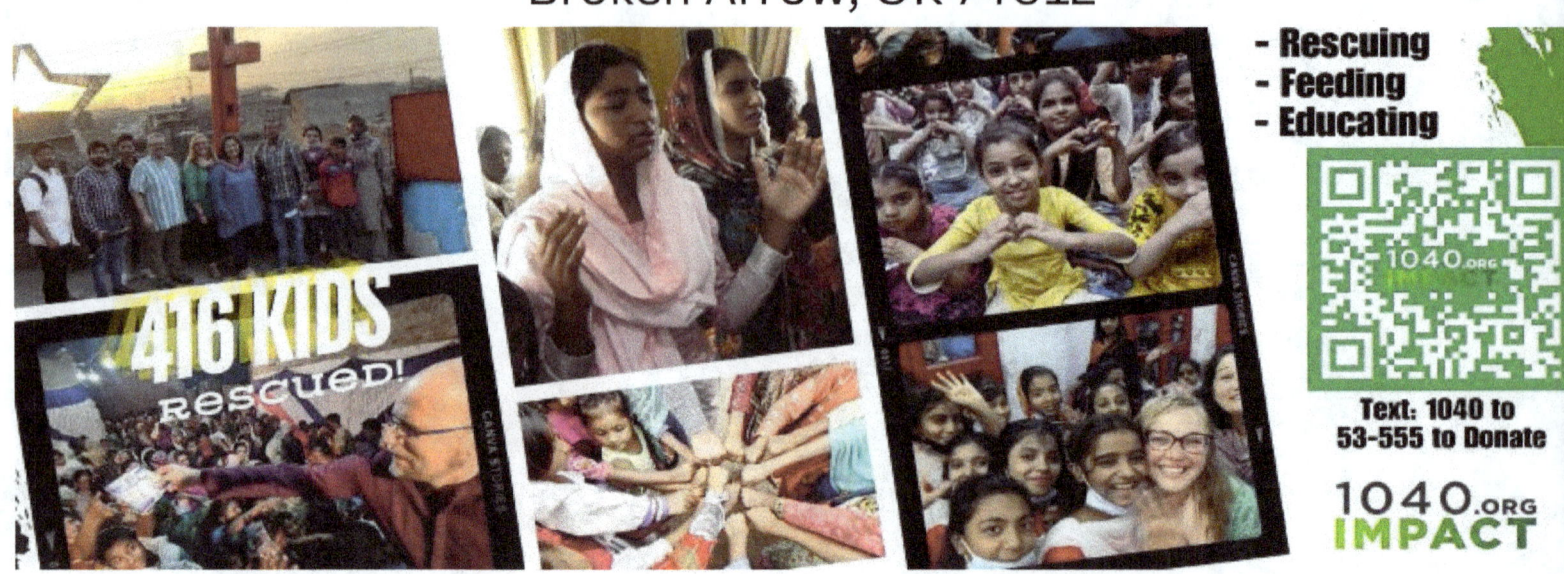

MICHAEL'S CORNER

Continued from page 1
*This Chirstmas I'll be in the USA with family, Pastors, Ministry Partners and meeting with our growing support network.
I'll return to Thailand in January to continue the work.*

A spring minstry trip is in the planning stages for Pakistan to visit our Pastors, our 4 safe houses and to see the new land we've purchased for our 4th safe house and discuss building plans with our team on the ground.

Every Christmas, we create a special celebration for all 416 of our orphans 7 years running!

Christmas in Pakistan

Every Christmas, we create a special celebration for our orphans who have been rescued from human trafficking.

December, we're gearing up for a heartwarming Christmas celebration and you can help us pull it off!
Click on the link and give us your best gift! Thank you and Merry Christmas to you and yours!

GIVEBUTTER.COM/1040CHRISTMAS

GIVEBUTTER.COM/ 1040CHRISTMAS

COMING 2025

ALL THE GOSPEL TO ALL THE NATIONS

THANK
YOU!

ISBN 978-1-63792-810-3

90000

9 781637 928103

www.ingramcontent.com/pod-product-compliance
Lightning Source LLC
LaVergne TN
LVHW081531060526
838200LV00049B/2277